Cheryl
Annual 2011

POSY EDWARDS

Meet Cheryl

It's a Cinderella story – a girl from a Newcastle estate is picked to join what will become one of the biggest girl bands on the planet. And the story doesn't end there – she marries her prince, and finds fortune and fame as a TV presenter and solo singer, too. While she has suffered hardships and setbacks along the way, Cheryl Cole has become Britain's sweetheart, a woman who truly deserves her own 'happily ever after . . .'.

Books are to be returned on or befor
the last date below. 920

7 DEC 2010	2 9 NOV 2010	1 DEC 201
	− 1 MAR 2011	2 3 DEC 2011
	− 1 MAR 2011	− 2 MAY 2012
	− 4 OCT 2011	− 2 MAY 2012
1 7 NOV 2011		1 5 MAY 2012
		3 0 MAY 2012

LIBREX

5

*I feel very fortunate. But I'll never take
it for granted because I have this thing
in the back of my mind that one day
I'm going to wake up back in Newcastle,
and it will all have been a crazy dream.*

A star is born

Cheryl Tweedy was born on June 30, 1983, and grew up on a Newcastle estate with her home decorator dad Gary, her mum Joan, sister Gillian and brothers Gary, Andrew, and Joseph. Her early life certainly was not as glamorous as the one she leads now – 'I remember living on baked beans, eggs and bread. I'd get a Barbie that was four years out of fashion from a girl up the street who didn't want it anymore. And I'd get hand-me-downs from a girl up the road.'

But like many young girls, Cheryl imagined a different life, one in which her parents didn't have to work so hard for the few luxuries the family had. And early on, Cheryl's mother Joan noticed a talent in her daughter that set her off on the road to fame and fortune. Before Cheryl could crawl, Joan entered her in beautiful baby competitions on the advice of friends, and Cheryl was soon winning awards, including Boots the Chemist's Bonniest Baby. This led to Cheryl being signed to a modelling agency at the age of just four, and winning an acting job in a British Gas advert when she was seven.

Dancing Dreams

Cheryl's dream, however, was not to act, but to sing and dance. When she turned nine, she won a scholarship to summer school at the Royal Ballet, but she didn't feel at home there. 'I felt out of place,' she remembers. 'I was the council schoolgirl among the privately educated. I wasn't bullied but I felt pushed to the side.'

Realising the world of ballet wasn't for her, Cheryl set her heart on becoming a singer. Despite her father's objections, she left school at 16, determined to follow her dream. She got a job singing at Gateshead's Metroland Centre, an indoor amusement park, but two years later it didn't look to Cheryl like her dreams of becoming a pop star would ever come true.

Popstars: The Rivals

Following the success in 2000 of reality TV show *Popstars*, which produced two bands who battled for number one in the charts (Hear'Say and Liberty X), the makers decided to producer a talent competition that would create a boyband and a girlband – and then pit them against each other to see who had the greatest chart success.

The Judges

The judges for this new show, *Popstars: The Rivals*, were former Spice Girl Geri Halliwell, pop producer Pete Waterman (one third of Stock Aitken Waterman, who launched the careers of popstars including Kylie Minogue and Rick Astley), and the then relatively unknown Irish record manager Louis Walsh, the man behind Boyzone and Westlife. Presented by Davina McCall, the show began looking for stars in the making at auditions up and down the country in 2002. And in London, 19-year-old Cheryl Tweedy sang S Club 7's 'Have You Ever?' and impressed the judges enough to win a place in the next round of try-outs.

'I was shaking, just terrified, and I could hear it in my voice,' Cheryl remembers. 'I can't watch it back because it makes me feel quite ill and I can't believe I got through!'

When the advert came on for Popstars: The Rivals I was really low, the lowest I could possibly get, and I just thought, what have I got to lose by sending off for an application form?

The Ups and Downs

The next hurdle was for Cheryl to make it to the final 15. First, the girls and boys had to spend a week auditioning further, showing off their dancing skills as well as their vocals, which Cheryl said in the Girls Aloud book *Dreams That Glitter*, was the toughest time of all. 'I was really emotional that week, one minute feeling happy and then just being nervous and unsure of myself and crying my eyes out!'

Happily, when she was called in to see Louis Walsh, he told her she had got through. But the auditions weren't over yet – those that had been chosen (10 boys and 10 girls) moved into the *Popstars* house in Oxshott, Surrey ready for the live shows, where the public would decide who would be the five members of a girlband, and the five members of a boyband. Joining Cheryl was Sarah Harding, Lynsey Brown, Aimee Kearsley, Chloe Staines, Nadine Coyle, Javine Hylton, Nicola Ward, Emma Beard, and Hazel Kanaswarn. But when producers realised Hazel, who was pregnant, would be too far into her pregnancy to perform on the live shows, they needed a replacement and contacted Kimberley Walsh. Then Nicola Ward also decided to leave, and Nicola Roberts was asked to step into her empty place.

★★ The Final 10

The final 10 were set, and over the next few weeks the public watched as Cheryl and the other nine girls, and the ten boys competed for the five spots in each band. Singing songs like The Foundations' 'Baby, Now That I've Found You', Shania Twain's 'You're Still The One' and 'Nothing Compares 2 U', Cheryl won praise from the judges and, a few agonising weeks later, Davina read out the first girl who would be becoming a member of new girl band Girls Aloud. And that name was . . . Cheryl Tweedy!

The Cheryl Quick Quiz

Think you know everything there is to know about Cheryl Cole? Take this quick quiz, and see whether the points you score make you a true Cheryl fan or just a wannabe!

1 What is Cheryl's maiden name?

a Cheryl Ann Tweedy

b Cheryl Sarah Tweedy

c Ann Cheryl Tweedy

d Cheryl Ann Cole

2 What is Cheryl's star sign?

a Sagittarius

b Aries

c Cancer

d Pisces

3 Where is Cheryl's home town?

a Sheffield

b Newcastle

c Manchester

d Liverpool

4 What is the name of Cheryl's first solo album?

a 3 Words

b 4 Words

c I Love You

d 2 Words

5 What is the name of Cheryl's husband?

a Joe Cole

b Mark Cole

c David Cole

d Ashley Cole

6 What was Girls Aloud's first hit?

a Fight For This Love

b The Promise

c Walk This Way

d Sound Of The Underground

7 Which movie would Cheryl have liked to appear in?

a Pirates Of The Caribbean

b Sex And The City

c Avatar

d Mamma Mia

8 Which band did Cheryl perform live with during their 2010 UK and European tour?

a Take That

b Westlife

c Black Eyed Peas

d The Pretenders

9 What's Cheryl's favourite food treat?

a Cereal

b Potatoes

c Chocolate

d Biscuits

10 Who's the most charismatic man Cheryl has ever met?

a Louis Walsh

b Ashley Cole

c Simon Cowell

d Dermot O'Leary

Answers on page 62.

How many did you score? Test your friends to see who knows Cheryl best!

0-3

We think you need to study up about Cheryl for a bit longer. Then you'll be super fan before you know it!

4-7

Not bad. You know your facts, but not enough to be one of Cheryl's biggest fans. Could do better . . .

8-10

Wow! You know more about Cheryl than she does! Well done, super-fan!

Here come the girls: a Guide to Cheryl's Girls Aloud pals

'I'm not sure that people can quite understand how close we are,' Cheryl has said about her band-mates, who were chosen by the public on *Popstars: The Rivals* to make up a girl band.

Kimberley Walsh

Born ★ November 20, 1981 in Bradford

First claim to fame ★ Kimberley began as an actress, appearing in an advert for ASDA when she was at school, followed by the role of young Cosette in the West End production of *Les Miserables* and the ITV series *The Book Tower*.

Favourite food ★ Thai

When she's not in Girls Aloud ★ In 2010, Kimberley guest-edited *Now* Magazine for an issue, sharing the emotional experience she had visiting Uganda for Sport Relief. She also joined Cheryl for a climb up Mount Kilimanjaro to raise money.

Cheryl says ★ 'Kimberley's the heart of the band.'

Kimberley on Cheryl ★ 'When I first met her I thought she looked young, sweet and innocent!'

Nicola Roberts

Born ★ October 5, 1985 in Stamford

First claim to fame ★ Nicola made it to the final 15 of *Popstars The Rivals*, but was then sent home. However, when it was discovered that one of the final five girls had to leave the show, Nicola was asked to come back and join the other four girls who would become Girls Aloud.

Favourite food ★ McDonalds

When she's not in Girls Aloud ★ Nicola has launched her own make up range, Dainty Doll, for girls with pale skin.

Cheryl says ★ 'I couldn't be in the band without Nicola. She's hilarious, I've never met anyone like her.'

Nicola on Cheryl ★ 'We were both from rough places and we completely connected. We shared a flat and it was so cool, but honest to God, it was a mess!'

Nadine Coyle

Born ★ June 15, 1985 in Derry, Northern Ireland

First claim to fame ★ Nadine won a finalists place in Irish *Popstars* but was then disqualified when it was found out she had lied about her age (she had said she was 18 but she was only 16). Louis Walsh saw her talent, though, and persuaded her to try out for the series *Popstars: The Rivals*.

Favourite food ★ Mashed or baked potatoes

When she's not in Girls Aloud ★ Nadine lives in LA and runs a restaurant called Nadine's Irish Mist in California with her family. She is also working on her own solo album.

Cheryl says ★ 'We have genuine respect for each other.'

Nadine on Cheryl ★ 'As soon as Cheryl's album came out, I rushed to buy it – she's my friend and I was like "Woo hoo! Brilliant! My mate's got a record out!"'

Sarah Harding

Born ✶ November 17, 1981 in Ascot, England (her real name is Sarah Hardman)

First claim to fame ✶ Sarah performed at pubs, clubs and even caravan parks in north west England before she auditioned for *Fame Academy* and then *Popstars: The Rivals*.

Favourite food ✶ Italian

When she's not in Girls Aloud ✶ Sarah has acted in the BBC drama *Freefall* and in two *St Trinian's* movies (her fellow bandmates appeared as a band in the first movie), and she is also a partner in a venture to open nightclubs in London. She has also modelled for Ultimo lingerie.

Cheryl says ✶ 'We loved getting dressed up and going back to school for *St Trinian's*. We had so much fun on set just messing around. It really was like being back at school.'

Sarah on Cheryl ✶ 'I'm proud of her, man!'

Stylist for a day!

Whether she's on stage or off to the shops, Cheryl Cole always looks stylish, cool and fashionable – no wonder she is often voted the Best Dressed woman in the country! But could you do better? Why not dress your own Cheryl, using the mannequins over the next few pages!

You will need
★ Coloured pens ★ Scissors ★ Glue ★ Glitter
★ Sheets of coloured paper (or white paper coloured in)

Instructions
Cut out clothes using these outlines and pieces of coloured paper. Colour them in and cover them with sparkles, or whatever designs you choose. Using the glue, stick your new outfit to the different Cheryl mannequins and she's ready to hit the town . . .

Chill Out Cheryl

Before she was famous, Cheryl used to wear jogging pants and baggy t-shirts at home, but now you're more likely to find her in well-cut jeans, and a pretty t-shirt or sweater. (And high-heeled shoes, of course!)

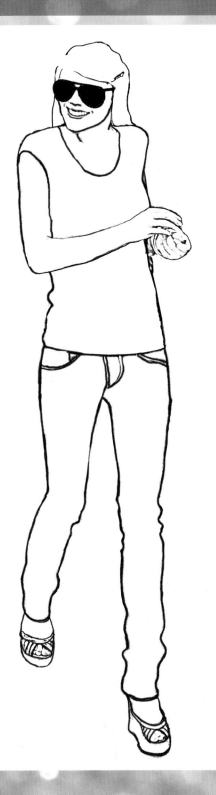

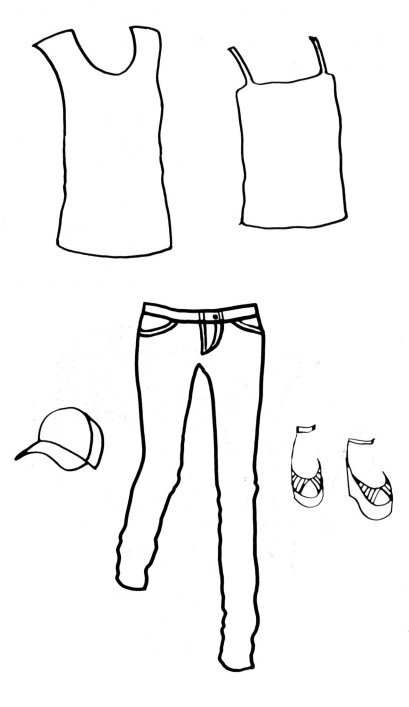

Pop Video Cheryl

We didn't think we would love slashed-thigh trousers, but on Cheryl they look great! Teamed with high-heeled boots, a black body and a military jacket and hat, it's a cool look that she's also worked on stage.

The X Factor Cheryl

When appearing on **The X Factor,** Cheryl has tried out evening and party dresses by funky new designers, with her trademark high, high shoes.

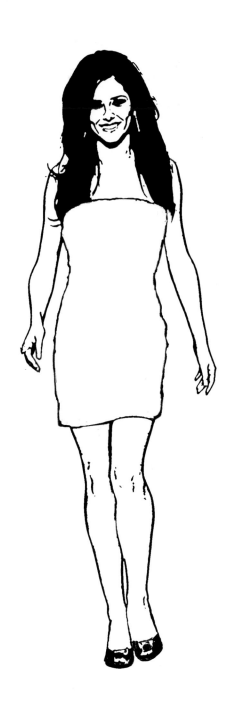

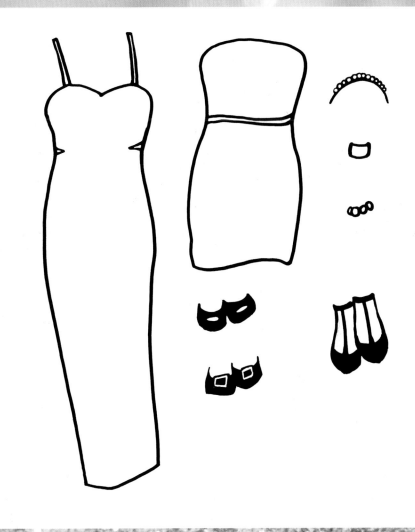

And how about you?

Find a recent photo of yourself, stick on one of the mannequins here and you're ready to dress to impress! Cheryl loves glamorous dresses with lots of cute sparkle, but try out whatever takes your fancy and create your own unique style . . . gorgeous!

Cheryl Revealed

Everyone wants to interview Cheryl. Here are some of our favourite quotes!

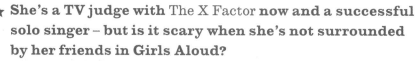

She's a TV judge with The X Factor **now and a successful solo singer – but is it scary when she's not surrounded by her friends in Girls Aloud?**

'It's exciting and scary doing my own stuff. Growing up I always wanted to perform, but I always wanted to be in a band because it's a form of protection being in a little gang.'

Would she like to be an actress?

'I would love to play a cameo in my favourite soap, **Coronation Street.** I wouldn't mind doing that, if I could just speak in my accent, be me in something for half an hour. I would enjoy that. But I can't see myself being an actress. I love music.'

What about starring in movies?

'If **Sex And The City** said they wanted me to be in their movie, I'm there. My personal assistant reckons I am half-Carrie, half-Charlotte. Not sure if that's a good thing or not!'

Did she want to be a singer when she was little?

'No, I wanted to be (ballet dancer) Margot Fonteyn. I wanted to be a beautiful ballerina!'

She's been a talent show contestant on Popstars. **Does that help her as a judge on** The X Factor?

'I think I'm at a slight advantage to the other judges as I've been in the process before. I understand how the contestants are feeling, especially when they are singing in front of us and a live audience of 2,000!'

Which judge does she agree with most?

'I hate to say this but I tend to agree with Simon! At the same time, I am more than happy to disagree with him!'

So does she get along in private with Simon as well as she does on camera?

'Simon and I think alike, and I'd like to manage some acts like he does. Someone said I'm a female version of Simon and I didn't know quite how to take that!'

Any secrets about him?

'I think he's really soft and not as harsh as people think!'

What does she look for in a contestant?

'I know it sounds cheesy but I look for the full package. I look for someone with a bit of sparkle about them, someone with the whole package as opposed to someone with just a good voice and nothing else about them.'

So what is the 'X Factor?'

'It's something you can't describe. Alex (Alexandra Burke) had it for me – that sparkle, the performance, the vocal, the personality.'

She's so busy, what does she do when she has time off?

'I like spending time with my dogs. I've got two chihuahuas, Buster and Coco. They make me feel chilled and homey. There's nothing like the comfort of your animals.'

And what does she do to relax?

'Watch *Coronation Street*. Order (food) in. I love to watch rubbish on the telly in pyjamas eating HobNobs. Nothing better. I used to be a massive fan of **The X Factor**, but I can't think of anything worse than watching myself speak!'

Earlier this year (March 2010), she climbed Mount Kilimanjaro for Comic Relief.

'No, just horrible! Except when there is a lack of oxygen (up the mountain) and you start to giggle about nothing. I did it because Kimberley (Walsh) wanted to do it.'

She's had a very busy 2010, with the climb and touring and releasing music. What does she want to do next?

'I don't set myself goals as in what I wanted to achieve by 2010, or in 10 years time. I feel like I've been lucky and blessed enough to have achieved what I have up to now.'

So does she have any dreams of being the biggest star in the world, have your own chat show or sing on the moon?

'No! I'm happy with my lot – anything from now is a bonus. Anything I do do, I'm going to give 100 per cent, I always will. But I don't have anything planned – I just go with the flow.'

Girls Aloud

Nicola Roberts. Kimberley Walsh. Nadine Coyle. Sarah Harding. Cheryl Tweedy. The five members of Girls Aloud had been chosen, but an even bigger challenge was on its way – did the girls have what it takes to beat the boyband (One True Voice) to the highly coveted Christmas number one?

Sound Of The Underground was a really good pop track. The boys had a rubbish song!

Number One!

The song chosen for them was 'Sound Of The Underground', a funky pop song that suited their voices, while One True Voice were given the ballad 'Sacred Trust'. By the end of the first day on sale, the girls' song had sold 60,000 more copies, and by Sunday it was official – Girls Aloud had won the battle of *Popstars: The Rivals* and were number one, not just for Christmas but for four weeks!

Now they had a number one hit under their belts, the girls had something to prove – that they were more than just talent show winners, they were a real band. Part of the reason for their success when other bands have fallen by the wayside (One True Voice, for example, disbanded after a year) was that they quickly became friends, with Cheryl bonding with Kimberley and Nicola in particular. And they all needed each other when on Christmas Day their tour manager, John McMahon, was killed in a car accident.

Hit After Hit

Kimberley, Cheryl, Nicola, Sarah and Nadine worked hard on their first album, 'Sound Of The Underground', which featured their first number one, and follow up single 'No Good Advice', a song the girls didn't like when they first heard it! It went on to be a huge hit, as was 'Jump', also featured on the album, a cover of the 1983 Pointer Sisters hit, which also appeared in the movie Love, Actually. The girls' hard work was recognised by music critics, with The Times saying the album was 'packed with everything you want from a pop record' and BBC News adding 'reality pop is not supposed to be this good.'

Behind the scenes, the girls had decided they weren't getting the help they needed from manager Louis Walsh, so they took over their management themselves with the help of Hillary Shaw and began to think more seriously about their style for videos and performances, and also how they handled themselves onstage. They began work on the second album with the help of Brian Higgins and the team from Xenomania, who had worked on tracks for 'Sound Of The Underground', and in the summer of 2004, the girls also unveiled a new look – toned bodies, well chosen clothes and an altogether more stylised image.

A lot of pop acts make a big splash with their first album and then fade away. We've done things the other way round. Our albums have got better and better.

Love Machine

By June 2004, they had released the first single, 'The Show' from their second album, and followed it with 'Love Machine' – a song Cheryl wasn't too sure about. 'I remember listening to 'Love Machine' and thinking we cannot put this rubbish out, that's what I said to the (record) label: 'it sounds like something Busted would do.' Then it went to Number 2 in the charts. So I was like, "oh right. OK. I'll keep quiet!"' She did the right thing – 'Love Machine' became Girls Aloud's sixth top three hit in a row, which equalled the record the Spice Girls had set a few years before.

Their second album, What Will The Neighbours Say?, featuring the Children In Need song 'I'll Stand By You' and 'Wake Me Up', continued the girls' success into 2005. With a new stylist on board, Victoria Adcock (who had previously worked with Christina Aguilera), and a Brit nomination for Best Pop Act, the girls embarked on their first live tour to a rapturous reception from fans.

Cheryl's Horoscope

Born on 30 June 1983, Cheryl is a Cancerian

Positives Cancerians like Cheryl are loving and protective of their friends and family. She's really sympathetic and a great shoulder to cry on in times of crisis. And, being imaginative, she's also great fun to have around!

Negatives Cancer is a Water sign which can indicate moodiness. Cheryl can occasionally be over-emotional, as we saw on **The X Factor**, but there's nothing wrong with having a good cry sometimes!

Friends Cheryl likes her friends and family around her – Cancerians love a stable life – and due to her kindness and sense of fun she has lots of friends to enjoy 2011 with!

Career If your star sign is Cancer, you are often creative – rather perfect if, like Cheryl, you are a singer and performer! Cheryl also likes to try new things, whether it's climbing a mountain or presenting on TV, so who knows what career path she will choose next? Things can only get bigger and even better!

Romance Cancerians are very romantic – a beautiful bunch of roses are a special treat as the rose is the flower for Cheryl's birth month, June.

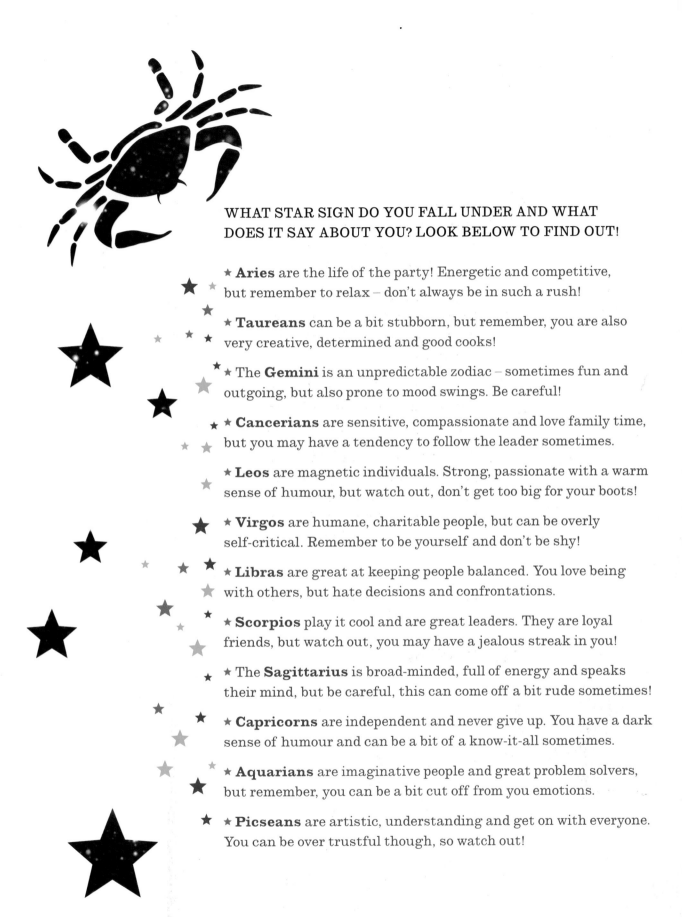

WHAT STAR SIGN DO YOU FALL UNDER AND WHAT
DOES IT SAY ABOUT YOU? LOOK BELOW TO FIND OUT!

★ **Aries** are the life of the party! Energetic and competitive, but remember to relax – don't always be in such a rush!

★ **Taureans** can be a bit stubborn, but remember, you are also very creative, determined and good cooks!

★ The **Gemini** is an unpredictable zodiac – sometimes fun and outgoing, but also prone to mood swings. Be careful!

★ **Cancerians** are sensitive, compassionate and love family time, but you may have a tendency to follow the leader sometimes.

★ **Leos** are magnetic individuals. Strong, passionate with a warm sense of humour, but watch out, don't get too big for your boots!

★ **Virgos** are humane, charitable people, but can be overly self-critical. Remember to be yourself and don't be shy!

★ **Libras** are great at keeping people balanced. You love being with others, but hate decisions and confrontations.

★ **Scorpios** play it cool and are great leaders. They are loyal friends, but watch out, you may have a jealous streak in you!

★ The **Sagittarius** is broad-minded, full of energy and speaks their mind, but be careful, this can come off a bit rude sometimes!

★ **Capricorns** are independent and never give up. You have a dark sense of humour and can be a bit of a know-it-all sometimes.

★ **Aquarians** are imaginative people and great problem solvers, but remember, you can be a bit cut off from you emotions.

★ **Picseans** are artistic, understanding and get on with everyone. You can be over trustful though, so watch out!

Cheryl on . . .

Find out what Cheryl thinks about Girls Aloud's predecessors The Spice Girls, being a role model and will. i. am!

The year after winning The X Factor
'The past year has been the best ever. I feel like I've got a fairy godmother watching over me.'

The Spice Girls
'We would love to have the same success as the Spice Girls. They really made it. They paved the way for girl groups and we'd love to think this is our time now.'

Body art
'I absolutely love my tattoos. The girls and I decided that the next time Girls Aloud have a No. 1, we'll all get one done. I want us to get something that only makes sense if we all stand in line, though!'

Chocolate!
'Sometimes I just feel like I need a chocolate bar. I don't deny myself anything.' Good for her!

Her collaboration with will.i.am
'I would work with Will for the rest of my life if I could. He is everything you would want from a producer, and also from a person. He's a lovely person. I'd work with him for ever if I could.'

Her first solo number one
'It's a pleasure to be here. To be No 1 is the goal. It's the best feeling in the world.'

Being a role model

'It's a lot of pressure if you allow it to be. I'm still a human being so obviously there's going to be times when I make mistakes or I make a bad choice – but I'm hoping that that's also an inspiration to women.'

Her body philosophy

'As I've matured into a woman, I've reached the point where I realize I've got to concentrate on my best bits rather than struggle and strive for things I'll never achieve.'

Going to ballet school

'I felt out of place . . . I wasn't bullied but I felt shoved to the side. I came back speaking posh and my mother was like, 'What the heck happened to you?' After that I didn't go back to ballet, I started singing after that.'

Girls Aloud: the Future

With five hit albums behind them, plus successful tours, a cameo in the *St Trinian's* movie and even a TV show – *The Passions Of Girls Aloud*, in which Sarah, Nicola, Kimberley and Cheryl all tried to pursue a dream, Cheryl's being to learn to street dance. But would it be the end for Girls Aloud now they had worldwide success and everything they could dream of?

Despite solo projects – Cheryl's solo album and *The X Factor* role, Nicola's make-up range, Nadine's upcoming solo career and her move to Los Angeles – the girls insist there is more to come from Britain's favourite girlband. At the end of their book, *Dreams That Glitter*, Nadine says 'I would never be into splitting up, I don't think we should ever break up', while Sarah adds 'This is my dream, I could never see myself doing anything else.'

We've been through so much, watched each other grow and learned from each other.

The X Factor

In 2007, Sharon Osborne quit her role on pop talent show *The X Factor*, leaving Simon Cowell and his team desperately searching for her replacement for the next series. Spice Girl Mel B and actress Amanda Holden were mentioned, but it was Cheryl Cole who Simon asked to sit at the famous judges' table with him, Louis Walsh and Dannii Minogue.

If at first you don't succeed...

In fact, Simon asked Cheryl three times before she agreed to the role. 'He kept texting me and texting me and texting me and, in the end, I gave in. I couldn't help it!' She laughs. 'Simon is the most charismatic man I've ever met – it's like he's trancing you or something . . . It's actually quite scary!' Cheryl's new job began with her attending the opening auditions for the series, and newspapers reported her every move, commenting on what she wore to each audition (and sparking a rivalry in the papers' minds at least) and whether it was nicer than what fellow judge Dannii Minogue wore.

The most nerve-wracking part for Cheryl was the live shows. 'I felt uncomfortable,' she says, 'then I started to realise I could actually benefit these people because I know how they feel. I can help them.'

Sharon's shadow was really hard to fill, and at the time my only impression of judging was of being judged, so being given that name was scary.

The People's Judge

Cheryl proved, of course, to be a very sympathetic and reasonable judge, and she became known for wearing her heart on her sleeve – there were more than a few tears during the first series in which she was a judge! 'I've just always been a sensitive person. When you've got a grown man in front of you on the brink of tears, I don't know how you can't be moved.'

Cheryl's emotional responses to the performances won over the hearts of audiences, and she became firm friends with the group of young women she mentored, among them Diana Vickers and Alexandra Burke. The rest, as they say, is history. Alexandra, with Cheryl as her mentor, went on to win the entire competition. 'I am so proud of Alexandra,' Cheryl said at the time. 'She is an amazing singer and I have every confidence she will be a world class star!'

✦ ✦ *In Demand!*

Of course, Cheryl's role in *The X Factor* wasn't over. ITV bosses realised she had made the show even more successful than it had been before, and her alleged rivalry with Dannii, and friendship with Simon, had made sure the series was always in the headlines. It was no surprise, then, that Cheryl was asked back to be a judge for a second year and she was thrilled to accept.

'I struggled at first in saying no to people,' she remembers. 'I think I may have given false hope. Coming back, I've learned more. I'm more able to say no to people that don't have what we're looking for and I don't feel as bad.'

In her second series, there were some changes to the format of the show – the most notable being that the auditions, usually just in front of the judges, now took place in front of a very vocal audience. 'I wasn't sure how I felt about the changes at first,' comments Cheryl. 'The new look auditions benefit not only the acts but also us, as the audience let us know if they think differently to us about an act and sometimes we change our mind.'

Mentor to the Stars

This time around, Cheryl was given the young boys to mentor, and called in a few pals to help her behind the scenes – her Girls Aloud bandmates. 'I don't have any choice in the matter, the girls absolutely love the show and all have their own opinions on everything and always let me know what they're thinking!'

It must have worked, as one of her group, Joe McElderry, went on to win the competition – making Cheryl the first judge to have her act win two years in a row! Now that's what we call the X Factor . . .

Dannii vs Cheryl?

When Cheryl was brought in to replace judge Sharon Osborne, the press speculated that there could be fireworks between the two female judges, Cheryl and Dannii – especially because it looked like Simon Cowell was flirting with Cheryl, and he had flirted with Dannii the series before!

While the two seemed to be facing off in the fashion stakes – magazines and newspapers each week judged 'style wars' between the pair, deciding which of the girls had worn the best dress – in reality there is none of the rivalry that was expected between the pair on or off screen. On Australian radio in May 2010, Cheryl commented on the rumours, saying 'Me and Dannii actually get on really well – she's an amazing woman and we have no rivalry whatsoever.'

Rumours

Dannii has been equally keen to stop any rumours of rivalry between her and Cheryl. 'People just assume Cheryl and I won't get on, but I don't get it,' she says. 'Why would I be upset that she's there (on *The X Factor*)? Just because she's younger than me? That's kind of insulting to both of us.'

In fact, the pair has bonded even more during Dannii's first pregnancy, which she announced at the beginning of 2010. 'I am absolutely thrilled for Dannii and Kris (Smith, Dannii's boyfriend),' says Cheryl. 'I think it's fantastic news and the most special thing that could have happened to them both.' And Ethan Edward Smith was born on 5 July 2010. So cute!

I find it such a shame that people feel the need to pitch women against each other. You never have Simon against Louis – it's always the girls!

Do Not Disturb!

Make your own Cheryl Door Hanger

You will need

★ A piece of cardboard (a piece from a packet of cereal works well)
★ Scissors
★ Glue
★ Two pictures - one picture of Cheryl alone, and one of her with Girls Aloud, like the ones below, cut out from magazines
★ Coloured pens
★ Glitter pens

Instructions

1 Draw a door hanger shape (you can copy the one opposite) onto the piece of cardboard.
2 Cut it out carefully with the scissors.
3 Choose a smiling photo of Cheryl and using your glue, stick it on one side of the card, leaving some space at the top to write "I'd love company, come on in!' above it.
4 Glue the photo of Cheryl with Girls Aloud on the other side of the card, again leaving space to write 'Do Not Disturb! We're having a secret gossip!' above it.
5 Colour in the curved part of the door hanger with glitter pens to give it extra sparkle. You could also add colourful feathers or stickers if you have some to make it really stand out.
6 It's ready to hang on your door!

Steal Cheryl's style

Cheryl Cole has gone from wannabe pop star to one of the most stylish women on the planet in just a few years. Whether she is relaxed in jeans or wearing the latest designer gown, she is always on trend, and wearing clothes that suit her petite frame. Here are some of her most stylish moments . . .

How she used to dress

Cheryl remembers what her style was like before she found fame as a member of Girls Aloud. 'I look at old pictures and I can't believe that was me,' she laughs. 'I went through a phase of being a bit tomboyish when I loved trainers and Timberland boots and baggy trousers.'

Out and about

Whether she's going shopping or travelling, Cheryl manages the casual look in style, combining skinny jeans and heels with vest tops, blouses, t-shirts or jackets. (And big sunglasses, of course!)

Daytime

During *The X Factor* auditions, Cheryl went for smart daytime wear, including mini skirts and little blouses, and a teeny tiny 3.1 Philip Lim candy coloured dress that was simply adorable.

On stage

When Girls Aloud performed 'The Promise' on *The X Factor*, Cheryl had more than usual to worry about. 'It was the most terrifying moment of my career,' she says. 'We couldn't walk in those dresses, and we were supposed to be dancing!'

Being a designer

'I would never want to design clothes,' says Cheryl. 'It's just not something I feel passionate about. That said, I would love to have a perfume – how amazing to have your own smell!'

The X Factor

We know we should have been tuning in to see the singers, but the best thing about *The X Factor* since Cheryl joined the judging panel is watching the battle of the frocks between Cheryl and Dannii Minogue. While Dannii often goes for long gowns, 5 ft 3in tall Cheryl likes her mini dresses, and wowed with quite a few. Our favourites? The structured red sequin Versace dress that looked like a lampshade and David Koma's 'dustbin lid' black dress that looked great when Cheryl was on stage but wasn't so impressive when she was sitting down. 'The alloy wheels dress was a bit of a disaster,' Cheryl commented to *Glamour* magazine at the time. Well, we loved it.

Her hair

'My long hair is a blanket for security. You feel glamorous if your hair is nice – if I cut it off I'd feel like I assaulted myself.' Cheryl has made a few hair mistakes in the past, though. 'When I was a teenager I got it dyed peroxide blonde. I didn't realise there were shades like caramel, I just wanted the blondest!'

Favourite designers

Cheryl's eye-catching outfit for the video and stage performances of 'Fight For This Love' was designed by Balmain, and featured a military style with those daring slashed trousers. A fan of body-con and glamorous sequinned dresses, Cheryl has rocked well known designers such as Versace, Roberto Cavalli and Matthew Williamson on the red carpet, while on *The X Factor*, she has tried directional labels such as Giles Deacon, Stephane Rolland and Richard Nicoll, as well as upcoming designers like David Koma and Beatrice Boyle.

Cheryl's Make Up Masterclass

Whether Cheryl is out shopping, performing on stage, or judging on *The X Factor,* her make-up is always glamorous, her look always fresh. How does she look fantastic, no matter what the occasion? Here are some tips to help you get Cheryl's look for your next night out . . .

What you will need in your make-up bag
- ★ Black eyeliner
- ★ Black mascara
- ★ Eye shadow – black, and grey/charcoal shadow, plus a pale pink highlighter shade
- ★ Blusher – light pink or peach
- ★ Lipstick – A neutral/nude shade of lipstick or lip gloss
- ★ Make Up Brushes

TOP TIP

'One of my key things is that I have to get my make up off,' says Cheryl. 'Even if I've been on a photo shoot all day and I'm lying in bed, I have to take it off because I feel filthy if I leave it on. I use a wipe first, then cleanser and then a moisturising cream before I go to bed.'

TOP TIP

Cheryl often wears false eyelashes – she even designed her own set that we can buy in the shops – but they are very tricky to apply and it's very hard to put them on without them looking wonky or even coming off, which isn't a good look! A quick alternative to false lashes is to use a volumising and lengthening mascara (and, if you think you might be going out to see a sad movie, make sure it's waterproof, too!) Apply one coat to your lashes, then give them extra oomph by curling the top lashes with an eyelash curler. Then apply another coat of mascara and curl them again – gorgeous!

TOP TIP

If you don't like the idea of a nude lipstick, try a clear gloss or one that's close to your lips' natural shade, but with a hint of pink. Don't go too dark, though, as you want subtle lips when you've got dramatic looking eyes!

Cheryl's Make Up ★ ★ ★

For *The X Factor*, Cheryl went for the dramatic, smoky eye make-up she has in her videos and onstage, flawlessly applied as the TV cameras were often close up to her. For a similar look, it's best to start off with a smooth base, using foundation if you want, or concealer to hide any blemishes or shadows under your eyes. If dark grey or black eye shadow seems too strong for you, you can follow the same steps using a soft lilac with a darker purple, or beige plus brown. Try out different colour combinations on the drawing opposite so you know where to apply the colour, and which one suits you best! (Lilac/purple looks especially good on fair skin).

To Get the Look

Before you start, apply some moisturiser to your face as it will help hold the make up for longer. Cover any blemishes or dark shadows with concealer that matches your skin tone and blend in gently. If your skin is shiny, lightly dust face powder over your face before you start your eye make up. Use the drawing opposite to perfect the look.

1 For smokin' Cheryl eyes, begin with the lighter of your two eye shadow colours – grey if you are also using black, lilac if you are also using purple. Sweep the eye shadow over your eyelid, blending the colour in over the lid and just above the crease.

2 Now put some of the darker shadow on your small brush. Starting at the outer corner of your eyelid, blend the shadow in towards the middle of your eyelid, and then up and out for a dramatic effect.

3 Using your fingertip or a clean brush, apply some pink highlighter shadow along your brow bone, and blend in. You can also apply some to the inner corner of your eye to get rid of any shadows but make sure you blend it in well.

4 With a steady hand, apply pencil eyeliner to your upper lid (use dark purple if you have used purple eye shadows, otherwise use black). You will get a better line if you rest your elbow on a table in front of a mirror to steady yourself, and start from the outer corner and draw inwards. Repeat for the lower lash line, but stop before you reach the inner corner of your eye. If you find this look too strong, sweep a little of the darker of your eye shadows over the liner, this will make it look more subtle. You can also soften the lower line under your eye by carefully using a cotton wool bud to blend it in.

5 Add mascara to your top and bottom lashes, starting at the base and gently working outwards to the tips.

6 Using a blusher brush, apply a small amount of blusher to your cheekbones. As this look has such dramatic eyes, you want your cheeks and lips to be more neutral, so only use a tiny bit, in a shade not much darker than the tone of your skin.

7 Apply a nude shade of lipstick or gloss to your lips, and blot and reapply if necessary.

You're now ready for that camera close-up!

53

Cheryl's love life

♥ *It's not supposed to be easy.*
It's not supposed to be perfect. ♥

Despite being just 27 years old, Cheryl has had her fair share of romantic traumas and successes. One of her first boyfriends, Jacob Thomson, was a carpet fitter she met during the *Popstars: The Rivals* auditions. It sadly ended when Cheryl realised the show's producers weren't too keen on the romantic developments between two contestants (although Jacob was voted off early on, the worry was that he was a distraction).

As Cheryl sailed through the auditions and became a member of the reality show's girlband, her name was soon linked with a variety of suitors, including Duncan James from band Blue and bandmate Kimberley's brother Adam. It was, of course, a young footballer named Ashley Cole who eventually won Cheryl's heart. To begin with they kept their relationship under wraps, but by autumn 2005 they were planning their wedding. Originally to be held at Highclere Castle in Berkshire, the pair changed their choice of venue when they heard Katie Price and Peter Andre were to be married there, and instead settled on Wrotham Park in Hertfordshire, and a wedding date of 15 July, 2006. But even before they said their vows there was trouble on the horizon.

From that moment on, poor Cheryl's marriage was under daily tabloid scrutiny. When she appeared on *The X Factor* without her wedding ring it made the front pages! 'Do people really think that I'm going to have an argument and take my ring off?' Cheryl asked a journalist in early 2010. 'It was more of a fashion statement than a marriage statement – look at the ring. As it's yellow (it's a yellow diamond) it doesn't go with everything!'

Sadly, in February 2010, Cheryl announced they had separated, her official statement simply saying: 'Cheryl Cole is separating from her husband Ashley Cole. Cheryl asks the media to respect her privacy at this difficult time.'

Going solo

While Cheryl was going through a very rough patch in 2009, she had something to keep her mind off her personal life – the launch of her own solo career. Working with Will.i.am, member of Black Eyed Peas and a renowned music producer, Cheryl recorded her first album, *Three Words*, in Los Angeles and London ready for release in October 2009.

The first single from the album, 'Fight For This Love' was a smash hit, with many interpreting the lyrics as being about her relationship with husband Ashley. When questioned about this, however, Cheryl simply replied 'It's to everyone that I've seen in a tough situation. I think anyone can identify with it. I hope it makes people feel able to fight harder and not to give up hope.'

Now I'm completely on my own. I wake up in the middle of the night sick with pure fear going What am I doing?

Another Record Broken!

The theme certainly struck a chord with music fans, as the song became the fastest selling single of 2009 in the UK for that date, while the album went double-platinum (selling over 750,000 copies) after just two weeks of release.

'Fight For This Love', which Cheryl performed on *The X Factor*, was followed by two more hits, '3 Words', featuring Will.i.am and 'Parachute', and her collaboration with Will.i.am led to her spending the spring of 2010 as the support act for Black Eyed Peas during their European tour.

With the album a huge success, Cheryl has hinted that another collaboration with Will.i.am could be on the cards. 'I would work with him for the rest of my career if I could,' she told Fearne Cotton in a radio interview. 'He's absolutely inspiring, fantastic, futuristic, creative, everything you'd want from a producer and a person.'

True or false?

Here are some statements about Cheryl's life. But are they *true* or *false*? See how many you get right and find out how devoted a fan you are!

1 Cheryl's first big break was winning a Boots The Chemist Bonniest Baby Competition before she could crawl.

2 Her first TV appearance was on **Popstars: The Rivals**

3 When she was little, Cheryl wanted to be a singer when she grew up.

4 Cheryl sung the S Club 7 song 'Have You Ever' at her Glasgow audition for **Popstars: The Rivals**.

5 Girls Aloud's first hit was 'Sound Of The Underground'.

6 The boy band they beat to Number One on **Popstars: The Rivals** were called Diversity.

7 Girls Aloud recorded the classic song 'I'll Stand By You' for Children In Need. The original version of the song was by The Smiths.

8 Cheryl and Ashley Cole spent their honeymoon in the Seychelles.

9 Girls Aloud recorded duet 'Walk This Way' for Comic Relief with Lily Allen.

10 Ashley is such a bad cook he once called up Cheryl on the phone to ask how to make Super Noodles (you just add water!).

11 Their fourth studio album, **Tangled Up**, featured a photo of the girls wrapped in string on the cover.

12 Ashley's favourite singer, John Legend, performed at their wedding.

13 Cheryl and Ashley got married at the same place as Katie Price and Peter Andre.

14 Cheryl replaced Geri Halliwell as a judge on **The X Factor**.

15 Band member Nicola Roberts helped Cheryl select her final three girl contestants for **The X Factor.**

16 In her TV ad for L'Oreal, Cheryl gets to say the famous line 'Because You're Worth It'.

17 Bandmate Sarah Harding's real last name is Hardman.

18 The first single Cheryl ever bought was 'Never Gonna Give You Up' by Rick Astley.

19 Cheryl would like a cameo role in her favourite soap, **Eastenders.**

20 Cheryl has two Corgi dogs, Buster and Coco.

SCORES

Less Than 10 Correct Answers

Oh dear. You love Cheryl Cole but there's still much to learn about her. Read this book three times, listen to her albums and you'll soon know everything you need to know about Cheryl!

Between 10 and 15 Correct Answers

Well done! Perhaps another read of this book and you'll score even higher next time!

More than 15 Correct Answers

Congratulations! You know everything there is to know about Cheryl . . . in fact, you probably remember more about Ms Cole than she does about herself. A true fan indeed!

ANSWERS

1 True **2** False. When she was seven she appeared in a TV advert for British Gas. **3** False. She wanted to be a ballerina. **4** True. **5** True **6** False. It was One True Voice. **7** False. It was The Pretenders. **8** True. **9** False. They recorded the song with Sugababes. **10** True. **11** False. The album had no photo on the cover, just the Girls Aloud logo. **12** True. **13** False. They had booked the same venue, Highclere Castle, but when they found out Katie Price was getting married there, Ashley and Cheryl changed their venue to Wrotham Park in Hertfordshire. **14** False. She replaced Sharon Osbourne. **15** False. It was Kimberley Walsh. **16** True. **17** True. **18** True. **19** False. She would like to appear in Coronation Street. **20** False. Buster and Coco are chihuahuas.

Cheryl Cole Crossword

ACROSS

3 In 2009 Cheryl became the face for this beauty company

6 Number of times Simon Cowell had to ask Cheryl to judge The X Factor before she agreed

7 Name of Cheryl's first album

8 Colour of her diamond wedding ring

9 Girls Aloud's former manager, also a judge on **The X Factor**

10 Name of the man Cheryl married

DOWN

1 Name of Cheryl's mum

2 Town where Cheryl grew up

4 Company for which Cheryl starred in an advert at the age of seven

5 Boyband rivals beaten in the charts by Girls Aloud

7 Her name before she married

The Future

So what's next for Miss Cheryl?

Rumours have filled tabloid pages for months. Will she be on Simon Cowell's new version of *The X Factor* in America? Will she launch her own perfume or clothing line like Victoria Beckham? Will there be a new single from Girls Aloud to take us into 2011?

Only time will tell. But Cheryl herself knows whatever comes next will be fine with her. 'Even if this all went tomorrow, and I just had my family . . . I'm happy.'

I never wanted to be famous – what drives me is the desire to be successful, because what's the point of being a failure and famous?

PICTURE CREDITS
All pictures courtesy of Getty Images.

ACKNOWLEDGEMENTS
Posy Edwards would like to thank Jo Berry, Jane Sturrock, Nicola Crossley, Helen Ewing, James Martindale, Katrin Smejkal and Rich Carr.

First published in hardback in Great Britain in 2010 by Orion Books an imprint of the Orion Publishing Group Ltd Orion House, 5 Upper St Martin's Lane, London WC2H 9EA An Hachette UK Company

10 9 8 7 6 5 4 3 2 1

ISBN: 978 1 4091 2316 3

Designed by Smith & Gilmour
Printed in Italy by Rotolito

The Orion Publishing Group's policy is to use papers that are natural, renewable and recyclable and made from wood grown in sustainable forests. The logging and manufacturing processes are expected to conform to the environmental regulations of the country of origin.

www.orionbooks.co.uk

ANSWERS FROM PAGE 12-13
1a Cheryl Ann Tweedy
2b Cancer
3b Newcastle
4a 3 Words
5d Ashley Cole
6d Sound Of The Underground
7b Sex And The City
8c Black Eyed Peas
9a Cereal
10c Simon Cowell

CROSSWORD FROM PAGE 60
3A L'Oreal
6A Three
7A Three Words
8A Yellow
9A Louis
10A Ashley

1D Joan
2D Newcastle
4D British Gas
5D One True Voice
7D Tweedy